LOCH
NESS

GRAMPIAN MOUNTAINS

Ben
Alder

LOCH
ERROCHT

STEWART

LOCH
RANNOCH

GLEN
LYON

ATHOLL
STEWART

GLEN LOCHAY

LOCH
TAY

GLEN
DOCHART

CAMPBELL

MacLAREN
BALQUHIDDER

Strathyre

Kippen

RIVER FORTH

STEWART

ALLAN WATER

OCHIL
HILLS

FIFE

LOCH
LOMOND

Stirling

Alloa

Dysart

Clackmannan

Limekilns

Queensferry

Carriden

Linlithgow

Cramond

Leith

Glasgow

Edinburgh

D0476131

to Ettrick Forest
(David's home)

First published 2007 by Waverley Books Ltd.
David Dale House, New Lanark, Scotland ML11 9DJ.

Robert Louis Stevenson's Kidnapped — The Graphic Novel
Adapted Text © 2006 Alan Grant
Illustrations © 2006 Cam Kennedy

All rights reserved. No part of this publication may be reproduced, stored
in a retrieval system or transmitted in any form or by any means, electronic,
mechanical, photocopying, recording or otherwise, without the permission of the
copyright holders.

The rights of Alan Grant and Cam Kennedy to be identified as author and
illustrator of this work have been asserted in accordance with sections 77 and
78 of the Copyright, Designs and Patents Act 1988.

Conditions of Sale
This book is sold with the condition that it will not, by way of trade or
otherwise, be re-sold, hired out, lent, or otherwise distributed or circulated in
any form or style of binding or cover other than that in which it is published
and without the same condition being imposed on the subsequent purchaser.

ISBN 10 : 1-902407-39-3
ISBN 13 : 978-1-902407-39-5

This book is printed on Gold East Matt Art Paper 180 gsm
Scanning by Castle Quoy Graphics & Design, Stromness, Orkney KW16 3AW
Lettering and page make-up by Jamie Grant, Hope Street Studios Glasgow G2 6AB
Printed & bound in China by WKT Company Limited

Scottish Arts Council

·EDINBVRGH·
THE CITY OF EDINBURGH COUNCIL

EDINBURGH
INSPIRING CAPITAL

edinburgh
(edinbʌrə) n.
UNESCO City of
Literature

THIRDEYEDESIGN

Alan Breck Stewart comes aboard the Covenant

CAPE WRATH

THE MINCH

ISLE OF LEWIS

Little Minch

ISLE OF SKYE

Territories of selected clans
STEWART

David Balfour's route

Sea route of the Covenant

KIDNAPPED

Being Memoirs of the Adventures of David Balfour in the year 1751: How he was Kidnapped and Cast away; his Sufferings in a Desert Isle; his Journey in the Wild Highlands; his Acquaintance with Alan Breck Stewart and other notorious Highland Jacobites; with all that he suffered at the hands of his Uncle, Ebenezer Balfour of Shaws, falsely so-called;

Written by himself, and now set forth by Robert Louis Stevenson.

Adapted by Alan Grant and Illustrated by Cam Kennedy.

0   25 Miles
25 Kilometers

ISLE Of Canna

RHUM I.

MORAR
ARISAIG

LOCH NESS

LOCH LOCHY

LOCHABER

Coll I.

ARDNAMURCHAN

CAMERON

Ben Alder

LOCH ERROCHT
STEWART

MacLEAN

Ardgour
Balachulish
Duror
GLEN COE
Glenure

MAMORE
LOCH LEVEN
Koalisnacoan

LOCH RANNOCH

GRAMPIAN MOUNTAINS

ATHOLL STEWART

MacLEAN

MORVEN

APPIN

CAMPBELL

GLEN LYON

ISLE of MULL

Kinlochaline
Torosay

Ben More

Scarbh of Mull

GLENORCHY

GLEN LOCHAY
GLEN DOCHART

LOCH TAY

CAMPBELL

Iona I.

Ross of Mull

MacLAREN
BALQUHIDDER

Earraid I.
Torran Rocks
Shipwreck of the Covenant

CAMPBELL

Strathyre

Kippen

RIVER FORTH

ALLAN WATER

OCHIL HILLS

FIFE

Colonsay I.

Inveraray

STEWART

Alloa
Clackmannan

Dysart

Jura I.

LOCH LOMOND

Stirling

Limekilns
Queensferry

Carriden

Cramond
Leith

Loch Fyne

CAMPBELL

Linlithgow

Edinburgh

Kintyre

Firth of Clyde

Glasgow

Isle of Islay

Isle of Arran

to Ettrick Forest (David's home)

ON THE FORENOON OF THE SECOND DAY, COMING TO THE TOP OF A HILL, I SAW ALL THE COUNTRY FALL AWAY BEFORE ME DOWN TO THE SEA; AND IN THE MIDST OF THIS DESCENT, ON A LONG RIDGE, THE **CITY** OF **EDINBURGH** SMOKING LIKE A KILN.

THERE WAS A FLAG UPON THE **CASTLE**, AND **SHIPS** LYING ANCHORED IN THE FIRTH; BOTH OF WHICH I COULD DISTINGUISH CLEARLY, AND BOTH BROUGHT MY COUNTRY HEART INTO MY MOUTH.

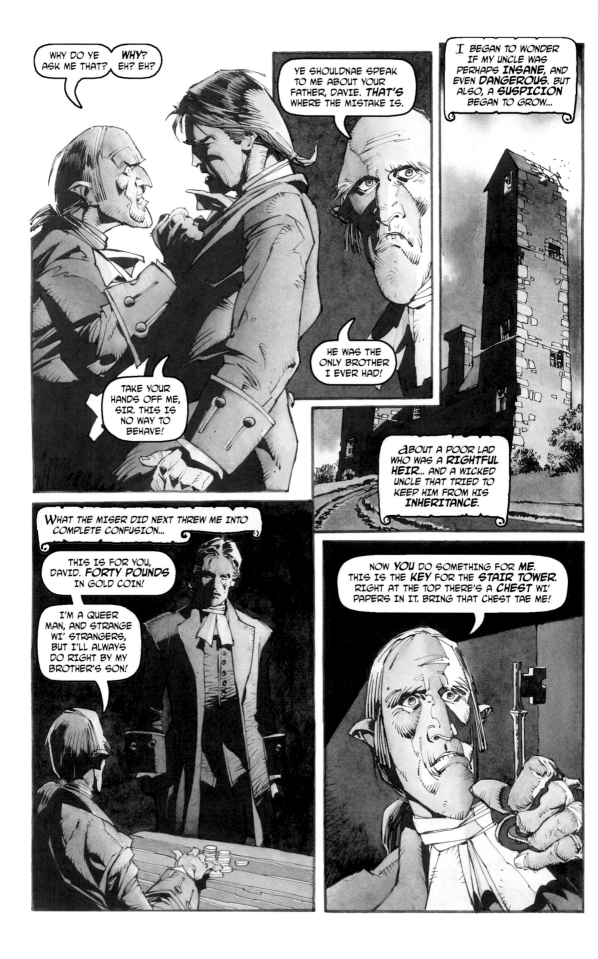

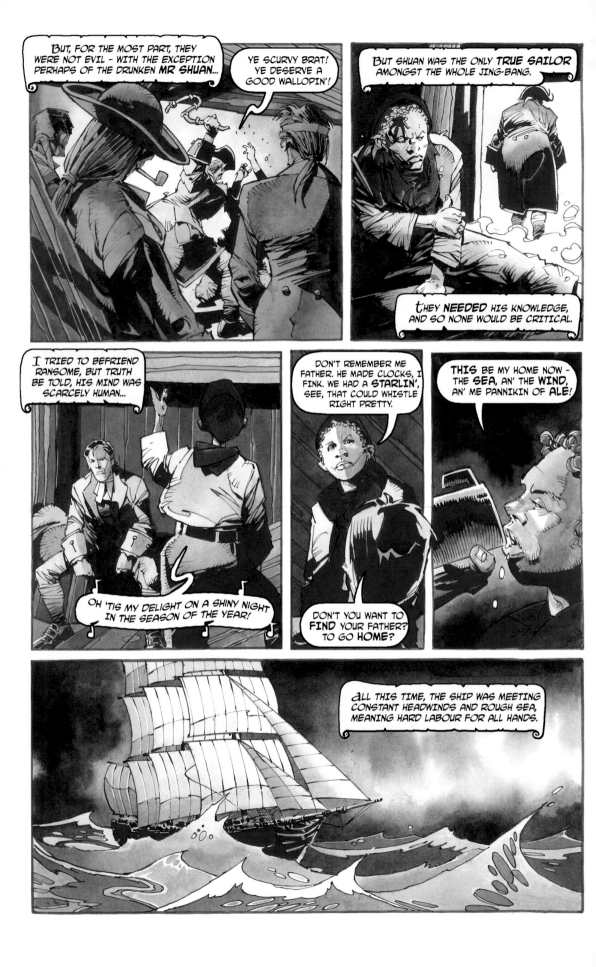

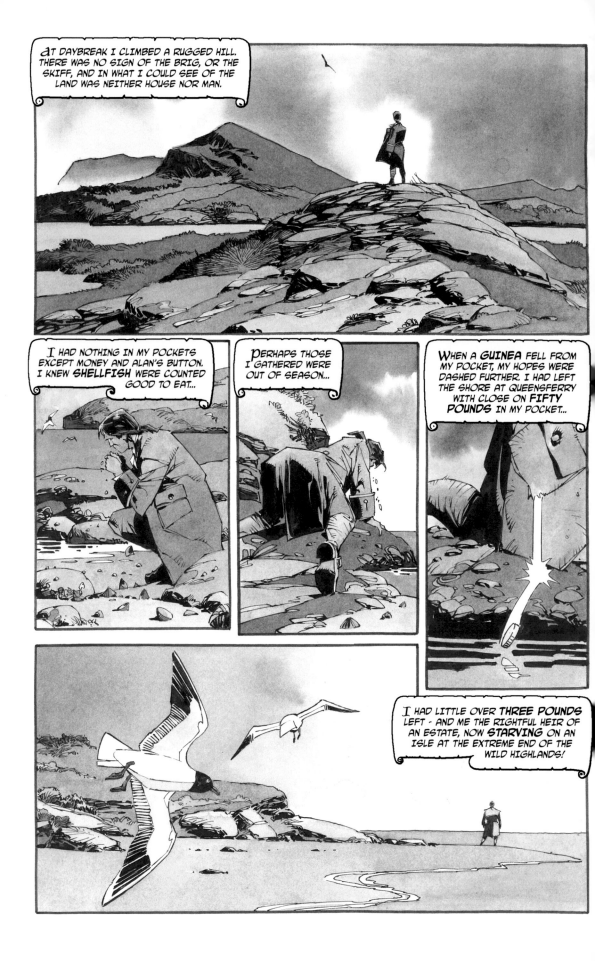

IT TOOK ME **FOUR DAYS** FROM EARRAID TO TOROSAY, A DISTANCE OF SOME FIFTY MILES. BUT AT LAST I SAT IN THE FERRY OF ALAN BRECK'S KINSMAN, NEIL ROY McROB...

IN THE MOUTH OF LOCH ALINE, WE FOUND A GREAT BOAT AT ANCHOR, AN **EMIGRANT** SHIP BOUND FOR THE AMERICAN **COLONIES.**

WHEN MEN LIKE THE **RED FOX** COULD GET NO RENT FROM THE PEOPLE, THEY OFTEN **STOLE** THEIR LANDS, AND **SOLD** THE HAPLESS FAMILIES INTO **BONDAGE.**

DAY FOUND US IN A PRODIGIOUS **VALLEY**, STREWN WITH ROCKS AND WHERE RAN A FOAMING RIVER. WILD MOUNTAINS STOOD AROUND IT; THERE GREW THERE NEITHER GRASS NOR TREES.

I HAVE SOMETIMES THOUGHT SINCE THEN THAT IT MAY HAVE BEEN THE VALLEY CALLED **GLENCOE**, WHERE THE **MASSACRE** HAD BEEN IN THE NAME OF KING WILLIAM.

IT WAS A BARREN AND AN EERIE PLACE, TRULY A GLEN OF SORROW.

WE LAID UP FOR NEARLY A **MONTH** AT THE HOME OF A MacLAREN IN THE **BRAES OF BALQUHIDDER**. HERE A **DOCTOR** WAS FETCHED, WHO TENDED TO ME CONSTANTLY.

IT WAS FAR THROUGH **AUGUST** WHEN I RECOMMENCED MY JOURNEY. OUR MONEY WAS ALMOST GONE, SO IT WAS **IMPERATIVE** I FIND THE LAWYER **RANKEILLOR**.

THE **BRIDGE** AT **STIRLING** BEING WELL-GUARDED WITH **REDCOATS**, ALAN MANAGED TO ARRANGE FOR US TO TAKE A BOAT ACROSS THE WATERS...

AND AT LONG, LONG LAST I CAME HOME TO THE LOWLANDS.

RANKEILLOR CAME WITH ME TO NEWHALLS, AND I WHISTLED THE **SIGNAL** THAT HAD BEEN AGREED...

WE TOLD ALAN - OR SHOULD I SAY, **MR THOMSON** - MY PLAN, AND ALL THREE OF US SET FORTH TO PLAY THE FINAL ACT...

NIGHT WAS FALLEN WHEN WE CAME IN VIEW OF THE HOUSE OF SHAWS. AS WE DREW NEAR, WE SAW NO GLIMMER OF LIGHT IN ANY PART OF THE BUILDING...

THE LAWYER AND I CREPT QUIETLY UP AND CROUCHED DOWN BESIDE THE CORNER OF THE HOUSE...

WHILE ALAN MARCHED UP AND BEGAN A THUND'ROUS KNOCKING ON THE DOOR...

EBENEZER BALFOUR! I WOULD HAVE **WORDS** WITH YOU!

NEXT DAY, ALAN AND I WENT SLOWLY FORWARD, HAVING LITTLE HEART EITHER TO WALK OR SPEAK. WE WERE NEAR THE TIME OF OUR **PARTING**, AND REMEMBRANCE OF ALL THE **BYGONE DAYS** SAT UPON US SORELY.

WE CAME THE BY-WAY OVER THE HILL OF **CORSTORPHINE**, AND LOOKED DOWN ON THE BOGS AND OVER TO THE CITY AND THE CASTLE ON THE HILL. AND WE KNEW WE HAD COME TO WHERE OUR WAYS PARTED.

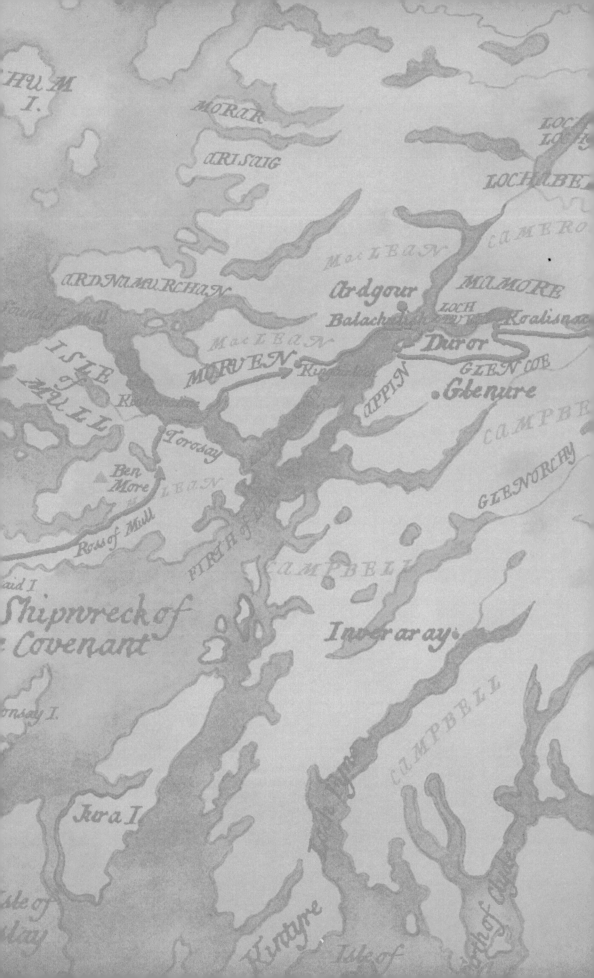